BIG AND Little

Samantha Berger
Pamela Chanko

Scholastic Inc.

New York • Toronto • London • Auckland • Sydney

Acknowledgments

Literacy Specialist: Linda Cornwell

Early Childhood Consultant: Ellen Booth Church

Design: Silver Editions

Photo Research: Silver Editions

Endnotes: Susan Russell

Endnote Illustrations: Ruth Flanigan

Photographs: Cover: David Allan Brandt/Tony Stone Images; p. 1: David Allan Brandt/Tony Stone Images; p. 2: Tim Davis/Tony Stone Images; p. 3: A. E. Zuckerman/Photo Edit; p. 4: Robert Brenner/Photo Edit; p. 5: Frank Siteman/Tony Stone Images; p. 6: Myrleen Ferguson/Photo Edit; p. 7: Rovert Van Der Hils/Tony Stone Images; p. 8: Nicholas DeVore/Photo Edit; p. 9: Susan Lapides/Gamma Liaison; p. 10: Jack K. Clark/The Image Works; p. 11: John Higginson/Tony Stone Images; p. 12: Roy Morsch/The Stock Market.

Library of Congress Cataloging-in-Publication Data
Berger, Samantha.
Big and little/Samantha Berger, Pamela Chanko.
p.cm. --(Learning center emergent readers)
Summary: Labeled photographs compare different
large and small dogs, houses, hands, sand castles, and more.
ISBN 0-439-04597-5 (pbk.: alk. paper)
1. Size perception--Juvenile literature. 2. Size judgment--
Juvenile literature. [1. Size.] I. Chanko, Pamela, 1968-. II.Title. III. Series.
BF299.S5B45 1998
152.7'52--dc21   98-54207
                                                                                                              CIP AC

15   16   17   18   19   20   08   09   08   07   06   05

Big dog and little dog.

Big elephant and little elephant.

Big bear and little bear.

Big hand and little hand.

Big bike and little bike.

Big chair and little chair.

Big leaf and little leaf.

Big boat and little boat.

Big house and little house.

Big tree and little tree.

Big sandcastle and little sandcastle.

Both the same size!

BIG AND Little

The world is full of things and they are all different sizes. Sometimes you need to use tools for measuring the sizes of things, but sometimes all you need are your eyes to see which is big and which is little. Things can be big or little for different reasons.

Dogs Dogs come in all different sizes. The big dog is a Great Dane, one of the biggest breeds of dogs. Even when it was a puppy, it was still bigger than the full-grown Chihuahua. This breed originally came from Mexico. Some of them are so small they can sit in a teacup! These two dogs are both fully grown. The Chihuahua will never be as big as the Great Dane.

Elephants We naturally think of all elephants as big, but baby elephants are much smaller than their mothers. The baby elephant, called a calf, grows inside the mother elephant until it is ready to be born into the world and breathe, walk, and eat on its own. Right now, this baby elephant is little enough to fit underneath its mother, but eventually it will grow up to be as big as she is.

Bears Here is a mother polar bear with her baby. The little bear stays with its mother for two to three years, growing up and learning how to fish and hunt. When the young bear is about the same size as its mother, it is ready to leave her side and take care of itself.

Hands These are human hands, and they come in all sizes. Big hands belong to adults and little hands belong to babies. Children have medium-sized hands. Just like animals, human babies start out little and grow up to be big. Their hands get bigger and stronger along with the rest of their bodies. What size would you call your hands right now?

Bikes Bikes are made in all different sizes because people are all different sizes. Very small children start out with tricycles that have three wheels. As children grow, they learn how to ride bicycles that have two wheels. Sometimes, small training wheels can be added to the back wheel

for balance as you're learning. It's a good feeling when the training wheels come off and you are ready to ride a big bike.

Chairs There are big chairs and little chairs. Mothers often use big rocking chairs to hold and rock their babies. When the babies get to be bigger children, they can rock in their own chairs. This little rocking chair is the perfect size for rocking a baby doll to sleep.

Leaves Leaves come in all sizes. All leaves start out little when they first come out on the trees in the spring. They quickly grow to their full size, but that size can be little or big, depending on the kind of tree they grow on.

Boats Big boats are made to carry lots of cargo. Many things we use are shipped from other parts of the world on very big boats. Little boats are made for sailing fun or fishing or getting just a few people from one place to another. If you could design a boat, what would it be for? What size would you make it?

Houses These houses are different sizes for different reasons. The big house is a shelter for a family. Several people live inside. The little house is a toy. It holds dolls and is called a dollhouse. Many toys are smaller versions of the real thing, such as toy cars, toy trains, and toy boats.

Trees Trees grow from tiny seeds. Young trees are smaller than the mature trees. They take many years to grow up, and different kinds of trees grow to be different sizes. This oak tree is very, very big indeed. Other kinds of trees are much smaller in comparison.

Sandcastles Sandcastles are just what you make them. They can be any size, large or small. Sandcastles are fun to build in a sandbox or at the beach. To build a big sandcastle, it helps to use a shovel and a pail. This is a very big sandcastle next to a very little one.

Same size Children are usually all different sizes and shapes. But these children are exactly the same size. They look alike, too. That's because they are identical twins!